BEGIN YOUR DAY WITH A SMILE;

Happiness Is The Key To Good Health

TABLE OF CONTENTS

Chapter 1 1
Chapter 2 1
Chapter 3 1
Chapter 4 1
Chapter 5 1
Chapter 6 1
Chapter 7 1
Chapter 8 1
INTRODUCTION 1

AF578833

All rights reserved. No part of this publication may be reproduced, distributed, or transmitted in any form or by any means, including photocopying, recording, or other electronic or mechanical methods, without the prior written permission of the publisher, except in the case of brief quotations embodied in critical reviews and certain other noncommercial uses permitted by copyright law. Copyright © ROSE OBENG,2022.

INTRODUCTI ON

Some of the time we make sensational arrangements that are supposed to give joy into our lives, whether it be an excursion, graduation, or wedding. But the straightforward delights in life are what we can rely on to give us nonstop satisfaction. At the point when we appreciate and partake in the basic things, the appreciation we feel will stretch out to different regions also. Here is a portion of the basic joys that merit trying to encounter frequently.

Newly cut grass is charming all around. The smell and feel of it under your uncovered feet are new and animate the faculties. Attempt to encounter this essentially a couple of times every year,

as the weather conditions permit it. What a superior method for encountering a straightforward delight for nothing? Give grins not exclusively to your companions, yet in addition to irregular outsiders, you pass in the city.
You will be flabbergasted at how great it feels to see first the shock of others, and afterward their grin consequently.
At the point when you sort out in an exhausting way, you will get an endorphin rush as a prize. These normal, lighthearted synthetic substances make certain to light up your day. Sort out in the first part of

the day to utilise this endorphin hurry to assist you with being particularly useful all through the remainder of your day. Regardless of whether your number one food isn't particularly solid, permit yourself to have it from time to time. The sensation of your much-cherished food will give you a little increase in joy. Studies have shown that on the off chance that you cease from specific nourishment for a specific time frame, it will be significantly more pleasant the following time you attempt it, so utilise this stunt to make your #1 dinner taste

far superior to normal
A few of us get by on our everyday espresso or tea. In any event, when it is an everyday propensity, it can give a lot of pleasure. As you taste your refreshment of decision, find an opportunity to partake in each piece.
This isn't just for youngsters. Put on some comfortable garments and essentially fall into the snow. Having a senseless outlook on this won't demolish the experience, simply embrace the sensation of blameless fun that creating snow heavenly messengers can bring.

Chuckling is like medication. Everybody ought to have a valuable chance to chuckle until it harms something like one time per day. Whether it is with a companion who could compose a parody or watching a decent film, get some margin to giggle away your pressure.
On the off chance that you have never had a back rub, check it out. This hour of all unwinding will cause your difficulties to feel like they are softening ceaselessly. Numerous people are even qualified for kneads through representative advantages.

Strolling in the downpour is one of life's astonishing basic delights. Dress warm, and go outside regardless of an umbrella. Allow the downpour to sprinkle over your face as you walk around, and make certain to hop in no less than one puddle just because. Costly tomfoolery is perfect, however, can be rare. Rather than hanging tight for your next getaway, enjoy one of these basic delights. By figuring out how to see the value in the easily overlooked details right close to you, you will track down extraordinary satisfaction every single day.

Chapter 1

Does Happiness Require Money?

As the idiom goes, ``Money can't purchase your joy." Or can it? Having an adequate measure of cash can unquestionably bring down pressure, yet having an overabundance of it won't make you more joyful than any other individual. Money means a lot to bliss. Ask any individual who doesn't have it. Having a higher pay, for instance, can give us admittance to homes in more secure areas, better medical care and nourishment, satisfying work, and more recreation time. We as a whole know all about the possibility that cash can't purchase bliss. However, we as a whole burn through cash, and for the vast majority of us, it is a restricted asset. How might we spend our well-deserved mixture in manners that will amplify our bliss? The mental examination offers a few helpful experiences about the associations between cash and satisfaction to consider before you make your next buy. Being Rich Isn't the Way to Satisfaction. Money means quite a bit of satisfaction. Ask any individual who doesn't have it. Having a higher pay, for instance, can give us admittance to homes in more secure areas, better medical care and nourishment, satisfying work, and more recreation time. Be that as it may, this main stirs in a limited way. When our pay arrives at a specific level and our essential requirements for food, medical services, security, and sanctuary are met, the constructive outcomes of cash — , for example, purchasing your fantasy home — are much of the time offset by the adverse consequences — like working longer hours, or in additional unpleasant positions, to keep up with that pay.

Doing Makes us More joyful than Having. A great many people expect that "things" will prompt more satisfaction than "encounters." Actual items —

like the most recent iPhone, purse, or vehicle — last longer than expressing hitting up a show, taking a cooking class, or taking some time off. Purchasing things satisfies us, temporarily. In the long haul, notwithstanding, we adjust to new things and even though they might have made us energised and cheerful right away, ultimately the thing turns into the new ordinary and blurs out of the spotlight. The joy that comes from buying encounters, nonetheless, will in general increment after some time. One explanation is that we frequently share experiential buys with others. In any event, when you've driven that new vehicle into the ground, you'll in any case be recounting stories with your loved ones about when you travelled to Colorado and you'll try and be laughing about when the vehicle stalled and you needed to go through the night in the obscure inn

Think about spending through Money on Others. The vast majority imagine that burning cash on themselves will make them more joyful than spending it on others. However, when specialists evaluate joy when individuals spend a yearly extra, individuals report more prominent satisfaction when they spend the reward cash on others or give it to a noble cause than when they spend it on themselves. This happens to pay little mind to how enormous the reward was. One justification behind this peculiarity is that providing for others helps us have a positive outlook on ourselves

Along these lines, before you take out your wallet or snap to arrange on the web, ponder whether this buy will truly satisfy you. Assuming it will risk your fundamental requirements, reconsider. On the off chance that you have some extra cash, take into account arranging an excursion or taking a class to get familiar with another expertise. At long last, in this time of giving, know that assuming you spend your cash on others or give it to great aims, you might feel improved than if you spend it on yourself.

Things being what they are, could cash at any point purchase your joy or not? The following are a couple of considerations to contemplate regarding the matter. Studies have shown that indeed, having sufficient cash to address your issues and those of your family gives joy. Individuals living in destitution are by and large less blissful than those whose needs are met. Having the option to take care of your bills and having to the point of scraping by monetarily will assist you with prevailing with regards to feeling blissful. Having more cash than you want, nonetheless, won't give you additional joy. Money and bliss are not corresponding. Somebody with enough cash to purchase a huge house and a few vehicles won't be guaranteed to have more joy than one more person with precisely what they need. There is the pressure that accompanies having cash. Whether you have a bit or a great deal, you probably have some familiarity with this pressure.

There is the pressure of realising you want to spend what you have admirably, as well as the way that individuals with ulterior intentions are attracted to monetarily affluent people.
It isn't really how much Money you make that guarantees your satisfaction, yet about the thing you are spending it on and where it is going on the exit plan. There are a few standards for utilising cash that can help you to feel more fulfilled. Where you put your cash and who gets it can have an effect concerning whether you acquired something by having had it.
Purchasing more things isn't demonstrated to fulfil an individual. Even though putting resources into things that will last appears to be a savvy move, it concentrates on a show that we will more often than not conform to what we get. Having these things doesn't keep giving limitless joy.
We are bound to have long-haul bliss when cash is spent on encounters that will give us enduring recollections. Whether this implies travelling without

anyone else or with your family or making time to accomplish something fun sometimes… make certain to make encounters as opposed to buying something that will just disappear over the long haul.

Giving is quite possibly the most fulfilling thing you can do with your cash. Whether it is for a noble cause or a companion out of luck, figure out how to offer in return and offer what you have. This is a method for spending that will bring long-haul individual prizes.

The short response is no; you needn't bother with cash to be content. Cash can be valuable, notwithstanding, to forestall pressure that can decrease the bliss that you do have.

Regardless of what measure of cash you have, utilise these tips to assist with accomplishing the degree of satisfaction you want, and carry on with a day-to-day existence overflowing with joy..

Chapter 2

Try not to Sweat the Small Stuff

Try not to perspire the little stuff" is an expression somebody might have let you know when you were furious, irritated, or stressed over something. You might have considered what it implied and what you should do about it.

We have all heard that we shouldn't perspire the little stuff. Allowing oneself to get worried over the easily overlooked details in life is one of the greatest ways of bringing pointless pain into life's way. We can stay away from a ton of pessimistic sentiments, and even medical conditions, essentially by learning not to allow the seemingly insignificant details to get to us. When something little happens that makes you need to seethe, contrast the second's importance with so much noise and distraction swirling around in your own life, and in your general surroundings. You might have spilled your cake player on the floor an hour before your visitors are expected to show up. Are your companions going to cherish you and partake at night regardless of whether you have a newly prepared cake for them? Provided that this is true, perhaps you ought to invest your effort someplace other than scolding yourself for this little mix-up. When something little takes steps to obliterate your demeanour and uplifting perspective, contemplate the way that no one's perfect. Whether it is yourself or another person who created the circumstance that feels like a train wreck, remember that mix-ups are a typical piece of life that happens to everybody. Try not to allow one terrible second to shock you. It tends to be difficult to excuse another person when it seems like they have brought you additional work and stress. At the point when somebody backsides your vehicle, you might be enticed to verbally attack them. Be that as it may, pause and believe about how it might feel to be in their circumstance. Try not to act and feel like you have never committed an error, yet pick compassion. Pardoning others can be a basic matter in contrast with excusing ourselves. There are numerous minutes that we treat ourselves more regretfully than we could at any point permit a companion to treat us.

At the point when you are struggling with pardoning yourself, consider how you would deal with a comparative slip-up made by an old buddy. Pause and think

before harassing yourself, and think about looking for proficient assistance if you can't

stop a fountain of negative contemplations each time you miss the mark concerning flawlessness.

We as a whole have issues, and by and large, at that point, any issue

appears to be huge. Insight isn't generally reality, however, and it depends on us to place what is going on into viewpoint so we can appropriately manage whatever comes in our direction.
When something negative occurs in your life, inquire as to whether it will matter in a decade. If it won't, let it go. On the off chance that somebody gives you the centre finger in rush hour gridlock, you might be enticed to freak out, however, it is just not worth the effort. Save your feelings for things such as reality-changing and merit your undivided focus.

When something turns out badly, you have two options. You can slip into a fury, or let it go. Pursuing the decision not to perspire the little stuff will give your extraordinary joy, and you will be appreciative of your own change in context.

Chapter 3

How Happy Are You?

Questions to Ask Yourself

A craving to be content is something that nearly everybody shares for all intents and purposes. However, it is generally difficult to find satisfaction, nor to conclude whether you are cheerful once you believe you ought to be in this specific perspective. Each life will have highs and lows, thus it is useful on the off chance that we have a check by which to decide regardless of whether we have accomplished satisfaction. This is an indication of your inward satisfaction. Do you get up every morning prepared to confront the day, or do you feel restless and unfortunate? It is hard to be content if you are getting negatively going every morning. Whether you are working, going to class, or accomplishing something different… you ought to feel a feeling of expectation when you ponder being there. There are sure things we should do, similar to paying the lease, so your choice to work may not be a choice. You do, in any case, have a choice concerning where you work. If you could do without it, transform it.

Individuals you invest most of your energy in are individuals who will have the best impact on you. Assuming they are mad, deterring, and need inspiration, odds are you in the end will turn into a similar kind of individual. On the off chance that your companions are not elevating, track down new ones. Invest your additional energy with the individuals who will make your life more upbeat, and will assist you with making positive recollections that will give long-haul joy.

A critical part of the joy is preferring and cherishing yourself for what your identity is. On the off chance that you don't, then you want to sort out why. Roll out vital improvements, and afterward decide to cherish yourself notwithstanding your defects. Bliss incorporates having a certain and secure outlook on your future. We live in dubious times, however, that doesn't imply that we need to experience consistently dread. Develop your trust in little ways, and think about directing assuming that you feel more than periodic pressure when you ponder the future ahead. Everybody has a day-to-day existence reason. There is something about you that makes you a special gift to the world. On the off chance that you have not found this about yourself yet, your confidence will endure, as will your bliss. There are numerous surveys and books devoted to finding your life reason. Consider money management your chance to find out more and find what causes you to feel most satisfied throughout everyday life. Being blissful is certainly not a silly longing. It is vital to know how you are wired and the stuff to be content with yourself and your life. By posing yourself these inquiries and afterward pausing for a minute to contemplate your responses, you will be well headed to the existence of genuine joy. Social researchers have invested a ton of energy concentrating on what satisfies us (and what doesn't). We realise joy can foresee wellbeing and life span, and satisfaction scales can be utilised to gauge social advancement and the progress of public arrangements. Yet, bliss isn't something that simply happens to you. Everybody can roll out little improvements in our way of behaving, our environmental elements, and our connections that can assist with setting us on course for a more joyful life. Bliss frequently comes from the inside. Figure out how to tame negative considerations and move toward each day with good faith. All people tend to be a smidgen more like Eeyore than Tigger, to ruminate more on terrible encounters than positive ones. It's a transformative variation — over-gaining from the hazardous or terrible circumstances we experience through life (tormenting, injury, disloyalty) assists us with staying away from them later on and responding

rapidly in an emergency.
In any case, that implies you need to work somewhat more enthusiastically to prepare your cerebrum to overcome negative considerations.
How it's done:
Try not to attempt to stop negative contemplations. Telling yourself "I need to quit pondering this," mainly makes you consider it more. All things being equal, own your concerns. At the point when you are in a negative cycle, recognize it.
"I'm agonising over cash." "I'm fixating on issues at work."

Indulge yourself like a companion. At the point when you are having a negative outlook on yourself, ask yourself what counsel would you give a companion who was down on herself. Presently attempt to apply that exhortation to you. Challenge your negative considerations. Socratic addressing is the most common way of testing and changing unreasonable contemplations. Concentrates on demonstrating the way that this technique can decrease melancholy side effects. The objective is to get you from a negative mentality ("I'm a disappointment.") to a more certain one ("I've had a great deal of progress in my profession. This is only one misfortune that doesn't ponder me. I can gain from it and be better.") Here are a few instances of inquiries you can pose to yourself to challenge negative reasoning.

To start with, record your negative idea, for example, "I'm having issues working and am scrutinising my capacities." Negative reasoning happens to us all, yet assuming that we remember it and challenge that reasoning, we are moving toward a more joyful life. Science is simply starting to give proof that the advantages of this old practice are genuine. Studies have found, for instance, that breathing practices can assist with diminishing side effects related to tension, sleep deprivation, post-awful pressure issues, wretchedness, and a lack of ability to concentrate consistently. For a long time yogis have utilised breath control, or pranayama, to advance fixation and further develop essentialness. Buddha upheld breath-reflection as a method for arriving at edification. Expounding on oneself and individual encounters — and afterward revising your story — can prompt conduct changes and further develop joy. (We realise that expressive composing can further develop temperament problems and assist with decreasing side effects among disease patients, among other medical advantages.) Some examination proposes that writing in an individual diary for 15 minutes daily can prompt a lift in by and large bliss and prosperity, to a limited extent since it permits us to communicate our feelings, be aware of our conditions and resolve internal struggles. Or on the other hand, you can make the following stride and spotlight on one specific test you face, and compose and change that story. We as a whole have an individual story that shapes our perspective on the world and ourselves. However, here and there our internal voice doesn't take care of business. By composing and afterward altering our accounts, we can change our impression of ourselves and distinguish deterrents that substitute the method of our prosperity. Various investigations demonstrate the way that composition and revamping your story can move you out of your negative mentality and into a more certain perspective on life. "The thought here is getting individuals to find a sense of peace with what their identity is, where they need to go," said James Pennebaker, a brain science teacher at the College of Texas who has spearheaded a significant part of the examination on expressive composition. "I consider expressive composing a day-to-day

existence course revision."
At the point when individuals get up and move, even a bit, they will quite often be more joyful than when they are still. A review that followed the development and states of mind of cellphone clients found that individuals revealed the most joy assuming they had been moving in the 15 minutes than when they had been sitting or resting. More often than not it wasn't thorough action but delicate strolling that left them feeling great. We couldn't say

whether moving makes you blissful or then again on the off chance that cheerful individuals simply move more, yet we in all actuality do realise that greater action remains closely connected with better well-being and more noteworthy satisfaction. Hopefulness is part hereditary, part educated. Regardless of whether you were naturally introduced to a group of miserable Guess, you can in any case track down your internal beam of daylight. Confidence doesn't mean overlooking the truth of a critical circumstance. After an employment cutback, for example, many individuals might feel crushed and think, "I won't ever recuperate from this." A confident person would recognize the test more confidently, saying, "This will be troublesome, however, it's an opportunity to reevaluate my life objectives and find work that genuinely satisfies me. Also, figuring out positive contemplations and encircling yourself with positive individuals truly makes a difference. Positive thinking, similar to cynicism, can be irresistible. So try to spend time with hopeful individuals.

Chapter 4

The Relationship Between Happiness And Food

Research has recommended that slims down that advance enduring bliss are those plentiful in organic products, vegetables, and other natural food varieties. Even though handled food sources can ease the uneasiness related to gloomy feelings, for the time being, research confirmed that enduring satisfaction lies in a sound eating regimen.

If you contrast the human body with a vehicle, food is very much like oil which is scorched to deliver energy. Without petroleum, the vehicle won't move. In like manner, without food, the human body will come up short on energy to appropriately perform. There are a few examinations that have demonstrated the way that craving can drive somebody to be mad.

Assuming you ask many individuals the justification for what good reason they eat, their reaction will probably be "to live" - yet in actuality, it goes past that. Have you seen that you get energised when you are presented with your number one dish? The simple sight of specific food varieties can cause the arrival of 'feel great' synthetics in the mind like serotonin. While there are logical investigations that propose there is a connection between food and temperament, especially bliss, the subtleties on how this is accomplished stay

hazy halfway because a portion of the reports has been clashing. About bliss and every region in your life, food can hurt or recuperate. By finding out about what food varieties to pick and stay away from, you will want to help your body and psyche, and embrace satisfaction.
So you need to utilise what The earth's life force brings to the table to help your temperament? Get going with searching for food sources that arc high in solid fats. Our minds depend on these fats, like omega-3 unsaturated fats, and they do ponder for mindset and further developing bliss by permitting nerve cells to convey all the more proficiently.
Pecans, pumpkin seeds, and fish oil are incredible methods for consuming these. Omega-3 unsaturated fats have been demonstrated to be essentially as successful as normal stimulant medications concerning gloom. Berries are one more awesome method for supporting your bliss. They contain anthocyanins, which are useful to your cerebrum as they support its

capability. Oranges, crude peppers, and kiwi are high in L-ascorbic acid which fights pressure. Mixed greens help your folic corrosive admission, and, surprisingly, dull chocolate is known to be a positive state of mind enhancer. Bananas and dates are effortlessly found food varieties that are known to influence serotonin levels emphatically.

Your mindset and mental capability are additionally incredibly impacted by drying out, so make certain to remain all around hydrated by polishing off a lot of water.

Sugar is the main food to stay away from assuming you wish to be content. Sugar sets you up for a speedy, misleading flood of energy when you feel the sugar rush, which is then trailed by an accident. Sugar can likewise hurt your insusceptible framework and trigger melancholy.

Espresso has been known to prompt tension, which will likewise deny you delight. Wheat keeps serotonin from being delivered, in this manner adding to wretchedness. Liquor is connected with ill humour, and albeit a few people feel briefly euphoric after consuming it, the inclination for the most part blurs into pessimism.

L-ascorbic acid has been displayed to diminish cortisol, which is the chemical that causes pressure. Except if you are getting a significant measure of this nutrient from your eating routine, an everyday enhancement is really smart. Since a lack of folic corrosive has been connected to discouragement, you ought to think about taking an enhancement. Omega-3 unsaturated fats and vitamin B12 are likewise useful for a characteristic state of mind support. Supplements that will assist you with controlling unfortunate desires incorporate vitamin B complex, Co-Chemical Q10, and resveratrol. Since food meaningfully affects your mindset, you should use it to its maximum capacity. Rather than simply picking your dinner in light of what you want right now, transform your plate into a strong weapon that will battle

sorrow and uneasiness, and construct and keep up with your satisfaction.
You merit the opportunity to feel satisfaction, and by altering your dietary patterns you can completely change yourself to improve things. Pick your state of mind by picking your food, and see the distinction it makes

Chapter 5

Yogic Rituals to Boost Your Happiness

As a yoga educator says, it requires work and loads of enjoyment to begin another daily schedule. As planned this stimulating Hatha arrangement so you can begin consistently with your satisfaction schedule. Put down the coffee and get your yoga mat - this is only the lift you want to remain positive and stimulated the entire day.

There are numerous ways you can build your joy, and a few stunts that don't need a lot of readiness or exertion.Our words have power, and by rehashing mantras to yourself over your day, you will discover that feeling blissful starts to work out easily for you. The following are seven mantras that, when rehashed frequently, can completely change you.

These three words can assist with keeping you from falling into a downturn of self-loathing. An excessive number of people don't have regard for them and fail to remember that they are astonishing, lovely, and stand out. Rehash this mantra frequently so the words will come to you when you want them the most.

Thankfulness is a certain method for acquiring satisfaction. At the point when you are appreciative, you are trying to help yourself to remember the beneficial things in your day-to-day existence. Thus, this uplifting outlook draws in considerably more beneficial things.

One of life's most significant illustrations is to adore ourselves. If you feel like you haven't exactly arrived at a mark of full self-esteem and regard, then recurrent these words until you do. Let's assume them when you are satisfied with yourself, as well as when you are irate and frustrated with yourself. Accepting that beneficial thing and positive circumstances are going your direction, will assist them with doing such. Considering yourself a magnet to all that is astounding will attract those things to you. Your fearlessness and positive soul draw in what they put out, and you will see your life becoming enhanced as you rehash this mantra frequently.

Indeed, even in the best conditions, some unacceptable individuals will hold us back from going the distance. Make circles that are confident and positive similar to you. Stay away from the show, and rehash this mantra to yourself when you are enticed to get sucked into somebody's negative energy.

Putting stock in yourself and trusting what you can accomplish will benefit you. At the point when you realise that you can do anything you put your energy into, you will track down limitless joy in that information. Express these words when you are battling to change what is going on, and realise that you have the power it takes to do as such.

Regardless of how much cash an individual makes or the amount they achieve, life will feel futile and void without a feeling of direction. There are a lot of books composed regarding the matter that can assist you with breaking down your life and figuring out what your particular design is.

Meditate the things you love and are attracted to, and what provides you with your most prominent sensation of fulfilment. You bring something particularly amazing to the table for the world, and this mantra helps you to remember that reality. Our words hold a lot of force, and mantras are an extraordinary method for showing us the way to joy. At the point when you utilise your words to bring positive things into your life, you will track down bliss. Rehash these mantras and figure out what a distinction they will make for you.

Assuming that you've been feeling down recently, it's justifiable. The world hasn't been the most straightforward spot to be in as of late. And keeping in mind that there probably won't be a great deal you can do about what is happening in the rest of the world, there is something you can do about what is happening in your inside world. Developing everyday customs that are committed to your prosperity and joy can be an extraordinary method for supporting yourself notwithstanding outside stressors.

Whether you're drinking some serotonin-helping bloom tea each day or conceding to a pottery class each Thursday evening, the accompanying everyday ceremonies are logically demonstrated to give you satisfaction and support. A ton of us know how to care more for ourselves, yet the hardest part can be getting it done. Assuming that you're battling to add health ceremonies to your day-to-day everyday practice, take a stab at booking them into your schedule or getting a charge out of them in reduced-down pieces. To practise more, yet can't focus on an extended class, do a 5-minute stomach muscle exercise and afterward continue onward on the off chance that you feel the inspiration to. Something else you ought to do is be extremely clear on your objectives and spotlight on a certain something. Rather than saying "I maintain that I should do more taking care of oneself exercises," say "I need to drink a mending cup of tea each day." Contingent upon the individual, utilising positive propelling prizes can likewise be useful. Perhaps you can indulge yourself with a back rub on the off chance that you figure out how to go to a yoga class 3-days per week. By the day's end, pay attention to your body and do what turns out best for you. A health custom that works for one individual probably won't work for another. At last, continually teaching yourself new well-being practices can be an incredible method for tracking down something that works for you! One or two investigations have shared the bliss-supporting advantages of yoga. One Harvard concentration shared that holding opening body stances for two minutes can assist with expanding testosterone, which has been believed to work on fearlessness and self-assuredness. The stances were likewise seen to diminish cortisol.

Yoga has likewise been displayed to assist with overseeing pressure, further develop rest, and increment energy levels, which all have an impact on your general joy. We love this 5-minute seat yoga routine since it tends to be added effectively to anybody's day. On the off chance that you utilise the Pomodoro strategy to work, this makes an extraordinary 5-minute in the middle of between 25-minute work meetings.

If seat yoga isn't for you, there are a lot of various kinds of yoga out there and we're certain one would work for you. The stunt is finding something you like and something that can undoubtedly squeeze into your timetable.
Time spent in nature is demonstrated to increment bliss. Even taking a gander at pictures of nature can invigorate the pieces of your mind which are connected to sensations of satisfaction, profound steadiness, and inspiration. While you may rush to change your telephone foundation to some florals or oceanside nightfall, there are more advantages you can get from really being outside.
Low degrees of vitamin D have been connected to wretchedness so by going out and getting in the daylight you'll be bound to get that sought-after vitamin D lift. Being outside has additionally been believed to bring down circulatory strain, work on your concentration, and even assist you with mending more quicker. Additionally, light has been known to hoist individuals' states

of mind. If you have any desire to get considerably more advantages attempt backwoods washing!

At long last, no deficiency of examination discusses the advantages of activity. Getting your heart syphoning has been displayed to help individuals unwind and encourage them. At the point when you practise your cerebrum delivers additional endorphins, dopamine, adrenaline, and endocannabinoid, which have all been connected to feeling less nervousness, feeling more joyful, and feeling more sure.

As we referenced before, simply seeing nature has been believed to help your cerebrum work better and assist you with feeling improved. In one review, understudies required a 40-second in the middle between the two errands. Throughout that break, they saw either a picture of a structure rooftop made of concrete or one canvassed in grass and blossoms. The gathering that saw the picture of grass and blossoms felt more re-established.

In any case, appreciating blossoms goes past that. Vogue as of late shared some narrative proof from a recent report where a specialist named Jeannette Haviland-Jones tried whether giving a candle, a natural product container or blossoms gave more pleasure. Individuals who got blossoms generally responded with a Duchenne grin, which is a grin that is referred to by clinicians as similar to the main sign of genuine happiness.

The justification for this may be that seeing blossoms discharge bliss synthetics like dopamine, serotonin, and oxytocin. These mind-boggling advantages could make them head out to the flower specialist, however partaking in some gorgeous entire bloom tea can give a significant number of similar impacts.

While our Shangri-La rose tea begins dry, after being lowered in serious trouble it will sprout into a full-bodied rose. After attempting a blossoming tea herself, Jessica Sullima from Thrillist said all that needed to be said when she said, "Envision the serotonin help you'd get in the wake of enjoying some time off from your screen to watch a solitary bloom sprout inside a teacup. There will never be been a superior winter to focus on small delights, and entire blossom teas are giving a solace that is both tactile and nutritious There are a lot of advantages to developing appreciation. One review uncovered that journaling for five minutes daily about what you're thankful for can support your drawn-out bliss by more than 10%! Life is generally difficult so it can get extreme to disregard every one of the upsetting things in our lives, however zeroing in on the positive things in our lives can be truly useful.

On the off chance that you battle by contrasting yourself with things you see on the web, appreciation could be something magnificent for you. One review showed that being appreciative of what you have can diminish envy and work with positive feelings. Rather than zeroing in on everything you don't have, with appreciation meetings you truly plunk down and ponder everything you are fortunate to have.

Assuming you're understanding this, all things considered, you are sufficiently favoured to have a PC and a wi-fi association and probably a rooftop over your head. This probably won't seem like a lot to certain individuals, however, there are a huge number of individuals who don't have something very similar.

Developing appreciation can be pretty much as straightforward as paying attention to an appreciation reflection or recording 5 things you're thankful for each day. Adding appreciation to your day can be a fantastic health custom that isn't very tedious.

Being imaginative has been connected to positive feelings and a more prominent feeling of prosperity. A new study revealed that individuals who took part in ordinary imaginative undertakings revealed being more joyful and empowered than when they weren't taking part in innovative undertakings.

Chapter 6

Character and Happiness

Character is the marriage of different words, your personality is the marriage of your viewpoints, perspectives, and sentiments to your confidence, convictions, otherworldliness, and values as communicated in your connections and encounters. It is the way you live when nobody is looking. It is the nature of your activities when there is no obvious advantage to acting great. It is the combination of thought, conviction, and activity into a cognizant character of the individual. It is the kind of person you are somewhere inside as an outflow of how you treat yourself as well as other people. It is how much you live with honesty to all-inclusive standards of fairness.

So character matters to joy. The establishment holds up the house.

At the end of the day, the character is to satisfy what an establishment is to the design of your home. Eliminate the establishment and the house begins to sink. Eliminate character and thus satisfaction. Derisive, mean, and childish individuals shouldn't be cheerful as scornful, mean, and self-centred individuals.

Of course, everybody wherever is intended to be content. Yet, nobody is intended to be content while participating in those ways of behaving, practising those convictions and perspectives, and carrying on with their lives in such a manner as would normally create its inverse of sharpness, disdain, outrage, and gloom. The accompanying personal qualities are those I accept will most assist you with living with more plentiful, steady, and brilliant. The most elevated type of modesty is the acknowledgment of our impediments - regardless of whether we recognize our boundless potential - while unflinchingly perceiving the reality of humankind's association and our dependence on a person or thing higher than us.

Lowliness is a tranquil kind of certainty, an internal strength that considers weakness because its holder thinks often more about what is valid than who is on the right track. Humble individuals are workable because, not at all like the pleased, they are available for analysis and rectification without being genuinely battered and wounded by what is said or even how it's said. Genuine lowliness requires profound strength and certainty, yet an internal development and close-to-home freedom of others' viewpoints.

It is in that inward strength that joy can develop to complete development. Modesty is likewise the doorway to fostering any remaining person attributes in that unassuming individuals are available to chances to learn and develop, to create and get to the next level. In that lies the mystery of modesty's effect on satisfaction: Lowliness prompts self-awareness. Self-awareness prompts more happiness.

At precisely that point where boldness flounders, is the place where any remaining person qualities bomb also. At the end of the day, fortitude is expected to nail every other person's quality to the mass of uprightness.
Adoring the loveable is simple. In any case, adoring the loathsome takes mental fortitude. Being faithful to your companions is simple before your companions. Being faithful when there is a strain to be backstabbing expects mental fortitude to remain valid. Genuineness, when you realise you will be lauded for talking, is simple. Be that as it may, genuineness when you realise you will be in a wide difficult situation for coming clean requires a wide range of boldness to tell it at any rate.
Facing shortcoming. Venturing into the unexplored world. Seizing a groundbreaking open door. Having a go at something you've never finished. Opening your heart after having it broken. Finishing the unpretentious toxin

of hesitation. Hopping into the profound finish of life. All such ways of behaving require differing levels of fortitude. Satisfaction requires all such ways of behaving. Constantly thankful individuals - those for whom appreciation is a lifestyle - are not just grateful for what the majority of us are appreciative of (an advancement, a birthday present, an outsider's decent deed), however, are even appreciative for examples covered somewhere down in the preliminary and deplorability of life.

Appreciative individuals notice the light in obscurity, delight in the miserable, and reason in distress. Where selfish jerks just see torment, misery, and vacancy, the people who have dominated the demeanour of appreciation see an amazing open door and completion and Paradise's directing hand even at those minutes it might seem we've been deserted.

They are likewise thankful for what others should seriously mull over the normal and normal - that which is so effortlessly underestimated. They notice the rose along the way and value its aroma. They grin at the interest of the kid who poses a large number of inquiries after questions. They notice the ripple of leaves in the breeze and the blueness of the sky and the freshness of harvest time. What's more, they feel the brilliant sparkle of satisfaction in each demonstration of appreciation they offer.

The cheerful is an open-minded bundle. They are lenient toward others' errors. They are fittingly open-minded toward their own (see #10). They endure the vulnerability of life. They don't want to control it or control others. They have toughness. They don't explode or make a huge deal about things. They can live easily with change and interruption and restricting thoughts and perspectives.

Love is the extraordinary neutralizer of pessimism. It permits us to see torment behind the outrage, to perceive stowed disaster behind extremely open articulations of harshness, and to connect with graciousness and sympathy to the people who strike out in dread and fault. Love genuinely vanquishes all. What's more, the cleaner the adoration, the further the satisfaction it produces. Unadulterated or great or unrestricted love is as of now not just a statement of adoration to a specific individual (my mother, my kid, my dearest companion), yet is a summed-up articulation of an inner state of the spirit. Pardoning at its most noteworthy structure is absolution comprehensively applied, as a statement of a generous heart. It is the mentality of absolution. It shows itself even as the offence is occurring. It is an unconstrained absolution. It's the demeanour of Gandhi to his jailors, and Jesus to his crucifiers. Furthermore, it is a personal characteristic of the profoundly cheerful.

The people who convey the heaviness of hard feelings develop to be abnormal and deformed with disdain and hatred. Be that as it may, the individuals who can lose such deforming weights of the spirit are lighter, more liberated, and more joyful.

Self-centeredness is the extraordinary destroyer of affection and sympathy, benevolence, compassion, and joy. The issue is that it is likewise a seriously normal piece of the human condition.

Yet, there is an oddity that is likewise, in some measure to a limited extent, an answer for the issue. It is at the point at which you lose yourself in serving others, that you truly begin to think of yourself on a lot further level. So remove the regular, yet devastating attribute of narrow-mindedness and figure out how to deliver and love and feel. Step into the sandals of others, see through their eyes and feel with their souls. Serve, favour, help, and watch the egotistical drive gradually channel away. Out of that help you render will raise a more profound feeling of importance and reason and satisfaction in living for an option that could be higher than yourself.

Be consistent with others. On the off chance that you say you'll do a thing, make it happen. If you don't know you'll get to it, don't say it. This forms validity. Others will come to trust and regard you when they are sure your statement is a more grounded cement to activity than a claim is a disincentive to being unscrupulous. What's more, as a great secondary effect, there is an internal certainty and euphoria that comes to individuals who carry on with legit lives.

Be consistent with yourself. Try not to seek after a vocation in medication when you yearn to turn into a designer or educator. Try not to permit the incongruence and disharmony that is the aftereffect of living clashing with who you in a general sense are. Be that as it may, who are you on a very basic level? You are an individual with monstrous potential, a man or lady who has the flash of heavenliness sparkling inside your spirit, who has mind-blowing stories of plausibility. Be consistent with that part of you.

Be consistent with widespread standards. Honesty to higher

qualities, to all-inclusive real factors, to truth, is our most noteworthy call. Misery is to a great extent the consequence of living incongruently to the truth. Some place inside every one of us is the delicate longing to carry on with an honest, higher, nobler existence. Something talks from our spirits, yearning for a long-term benefit and the blessed. We can hear it murmur when we're sufficiently peaceful to hear it. Cheerful individuals are the people who live more without fail to those standards.

Whenever difficult situations arise, what do you do? Do you plunk down, job over, and pretend to be dead? Or on the other hand, do you lock in, straighten out, hit the gas, and blow through hindrances?

The way to satisfaction is generously sprinkled with hindrances of trouble and challenge, of hardship and distress and agony. The individuals who continue, who persist and persevere, these are they who are the most joyful among us. They accomplish more and accomplish more and defeat more. Why? Basic: They don't surrender; they continue. What do I mean by being eagerly persistent? Maybe it is best put along these lines: Be anxious enough with life that you run more than rest, that you climb more than fall, that you learn more than pack, that you snicker more than cry, that you live more than biting the dust.

Show restraint toward yourself as you permit yourself the space to learn … and permit yourself to out and fall … and permit yourself ease up on your feet to get over yourself … and create … and improve … and advance … and develop. Also, show restraint enough with others that you affirm and approve and adore them in any event, when they are not satisfying who you realise they can be. Being eagerly persistent is the persistence that considers botches, however, doesn't make do with where you fall. It grins when you stagger, then pursues a little quicker recuperating balance for the sheer delight of the run. It's tolerating life's ups and downs while still living with enthusiasm, anticipating challenge and opportunity, in some cases simultaneously, and in some cases one through the other. It is the specialty of all while tolerating the normal part of defective mankind and perceiving the potential for something astounding in every single one of us simultaneously.

Chapter 7

Why Living at the Time Makes You More joyful

Do you, in the same way as other individuals, have a psychological rundown of things you assume you want to be genuinely blissful? There are numerous facades our general public helps us to pursue: achievement, abundance, distinction, power, great looks, and heartfelt love. Be that as it may, would they say they are the keys to joy? The exploration says no, essentially about long-haul joy. A renowned honour, a major raise, an intriguing new relationship, an extravagant new vehicle, or getting thinner, these things can encourage us from the get-go, yet the rush doesn't keep going extremely lengthy. People rush to adjust to new conditions — a quality that has helped us make due and flourish. In any case, it additionally implies that the positive things that at first make us more joyful before long become our new ordinary and we return to our old satisfaction gauge. Nonetheless, scientists in the field of positive brain science have found that you can truly build your joy and by and large fulfilment with life — and it doesn't need a triumphant lottery ticket or another exceptional difference in conditions. The stuff is an inward significant impact of viewpoint and mentality. Furthermore, that is uplifting news, since it's something anybody can do. We as a whole realise that living in the past can drag an individual down, however, why? Also, what might be said about living from now on?

We want balance, however, living at the time is something we should zero in on assuming we are to carry on with cheerful existences. Living at the time has been demonstrated to be the most effective way to become and remain blissful. Here is the reason. Pretty much all of us have lamented about something from quite a while ago, however, there is no way to transform it. Rather than squandering our minutes and energy in mourning over circumstances that are a distant memory and as of now not in that frame of mind to transform, we can utilise the energy to improve what is happening. Gain your best from an earlier time, and afterward continue. Try not to stress over the future, since you can't anticipate what it will bring. You can plan somewhat, and being unfortunate about what tomorrow holds will just goal stress that will add to wellbeing and mental issues. Live at the time and decide to make the present your concentration. Rather than dreading what repercussions your decisions will bring to your future, settle on choices given what is great in your life right now as of now. This will decrease inclinations towards misery and dread.

At the point when we contemplate the past or the future rather than the present, we float away based on common decency before our eyes. Perhaps your present includes a work project that requests your complete focus and energy. Perhaps your present includes little youngsters with runny noses who need lunch put on the table.

At the point when you embrace your present completely, you will get more out of the existence you have. You can at last quit undermining your current bliss with dread about what might come straight away, or the responsibility of choices that are presently before. Be grateful for the countenances before you now, and for the open doors that are thumping on your entryway at present. The minutes you figure out how to love will upgrade your future with the warm recollections you will convey there, and you will regret nothing over the lost centre. It's unpleasant when you're stressed over cash. To be content, you do require enough of it to cover your fundamental necessities: things like food, asylum, and attire. Be that as it may, when you have sufficient cash to be open to, getting more cash won't make a big deal about a distinction in how blissful you are. For instance, investigations of lottery champs show that after a generally brief timeframe, they are no more joyful than they were before their success. Being in a sound, strong love relationship adds to bliss, yet it isn't the case that you can't be cheerful and satisfied assuming you're single. For sure, singles who have significant fellowships and pursuits are more joyful than individuals in crisscrossed close connections. It's likewise vital to take note that even a decent marriage or heartfelt association doesn't prompt super durable, extreme bliss help. Anticipating that your accomplice should convey your joyfully ever-after may hurt the relationship over the long haul. You — not your accomplice or your relatives — are answerable for your joy.

It means a lot to Embrace the here and now. Having a reasonable centre is significant as well. At the point when you ponder the future, make the arrangements that are important for you to partake in that time later because sometime the future will be your "at the time." Don't disregard your making arrangements for the future, however, don't allow it to consume your life in an undesirable manner. Balance is critical, and will help you not to feel pressure due to a lot of spotlight on one region.

Living at the time is perhaps the best thing you can accomplish for yourself. Joy is accomplished when we decide to reside and appreciate where we are at this moment, rather than pining away for some other general setting. By using the time and the existence you are given very much present, you will know genuine satisfaction.

Chapter 8

Hormones and Happiness

Dopamine Frequently called the "blissful chemical," dopamine brings about sensations of prosperity. An essential driver of the mind's prize framework, it spikes when we experience something pleasurable

Whether you're experiencing Coronavirus exhaustion or feeling blue because of the dismal climate, there are a lot of ways of developing more bliss in your routine. The key is sorting out which exercises support your body's normal inspirational chemicals and accomplishing a greater amount of them.

"A variety of chemicals and synapses can assist us with feeling much improved, "And there are a lot of ways of setting off the arrival of these chemicals.`` As a matter of fact, straightforward exercises like activity, investing energy outside, and nestling with a little dog (or an individual) can get the job done.

Chemicals go about as couriers for our bodies, directing everything from our actual working to our close-to-home prosperity. The cool thing about large numbers of these chemicals? They're exceptionally affected by our viewpoints, exercises, and, surprisingly, the food varieties we eat. Understanding these synthetic substances and how they work can assist you with formulating explicit methodologies to feel improved.

Dopamine: Frequently called the "cheerful chemical," dopamine brings about sensations of prosperity. An essential driver of the mind's prize framework, it spikes when we experience something pleasurable. Applauded at work? You'll get a dopamine hit. Falling head over heels? Your dopamine levels will soar. "Dopamine creates that high we get from food, sex, shopping, essentially any movement that we view as charming,

Serotonin: Named the "vibe great chemical," serotonin assumes a critical part in fighting off nervousness and gloom. The primary class of medications used to treat these circumstances — SSRIs (specific serotonin reuptake inhibitors) — increment serotonin levels in the cerebrum. Working out, investing energy outside, and getting a decent night's rest can assist with supporting serotonin.

Endorphins: Generally regularly connected with workout, endorphins are related to "sprinter's high." "Cardiovascular activity is one of the most amazing ways of expanding endorphins. These strong chemicals go about as normal pain relievers, limiting uneasiness and augmenting delight. They're a key motivation behind why competitors can push past torment during an intense race or major game.

Oxytocin: Most popular for its part in holding and connection, oxytocin floods a lady's framework during labour and keeping in mind that nursing. Yet, conveying a child isn't the best way to get a surge of oxytocin. This "adoration chemical" additionally spikes with any kind of private touch, including clasping hands, snuggling, kissing, back rub, and sex.

Chemicals... they positively don't get a lot of regard on occasion. What do indeed

Do they have to do with satisfaction?

In reality, chemicals assume a major part in this inclination, and we are shrewd to find out what factors play around here and how we might profit from them.

Chemicals are extraordinary substance couriers that control a large portion of the body's cycles. The endocrine organs make these unique couriers and our body depends on them to appropriately work.

How we treat our bodies and the substances we encircle ourselves with affect how these chemicals can help us. By realising what they do and how we can help them in taking care of their business, we will be nearer to our objective of satisfaction.

There are a few chemicals that can help one's satisfaction. The primary ones
incorporate serotonin, oxytocin, and dopamine.
Serotonin has become very notable as of late. It is a synapse, which takes messages starting with one piece of the mind and then onto the next. Serotonin is vital in forestalling wretchedness and other dysfunctional behaviour, and issues happen when you have either a lack of this chemical or when taking care of its business can't.
Oxytocin is known as the "affection chemical" and has different positions, which incorporate assisting individuals with working on their interactive abilities and limiting trepidation.
Dopamine is another synapse, and it is enacted when a positive and unforeseen situation occurs - which is the reason it is known for its part in assisting the mind with finding out about remunerations.
Chemicals need to keep a fine equilibrium to permit you to work at ideal levels. To an extreme or excessively tad of any

chemical will cause short-and long haul issues well being-wise. Since our joy is reliant upon this, we are shrewd to give our all to track down a good arrangement for every one of the chemicals in our body, to establish a climate that supports feeling better. Significant ways of keeping your chemicals in great equilibrium and working request are to get adequate rest every evening, work out routinely and kill poisons from your day-to-day existence. Limit pressure in your life however much as could be expected, and keep away from conception prevention pills if conceivable. Food assumes a significant part yet to be determined of chemicals. There are numerous food sources that you ought to try eating consistently, and numerous you ought to endeavour to stay away from.

Food varieties and supplements that assist your body with adjusting chemicals and keep you cheerful incorporate sound fats, for example, those found in coconut oil, avocados, nuts, and wild salmon. Vitamin D is a significant enhancement, as is magnesium. An adequate measure of clean proteins ought to be eaten, as well as a lot of vegetables.

Your chemicals assume a fundamental part in your sensations of satisfaction. Keeping them adjusted and working for you appropriately is significant to guarantee sensations of mental well-being. By keeping the rules above, you will want to adjust your chemicals and carry on with an existence of joy and fulfilment.

www.ingramcontent.com/pod-product-compliance
Lightning Source LLC
LaVergne TN
LVHW050331160826
845677LV00014B/3586

9798849956701